Making Our Electricity

We can make electricity.

3

Look at the **coal.**

5

The coal can make electricity.

Look at the **wind.**

Look at the water.

Look at the sun.

The wind can make electricity.

11

The water can make electricity.

The sun can make electricity too

14

Glossary

coal

wind